Rules of
Church Work

Walking Worthy

(2nd Edition)

Dag Heward-Mills

Parchment House

RULES OF CHURCH WORK (2ND EDITION)

Copyright © 2019 Dag Heward-Mills

First Edition published 2008 by Lux Verbi (Pty) Ltd. 2008
3rd printing 2011
ISBN: 978-9988-596-73-6

Second Edition published 2019 by Parchment House
2nd Printing 2020

[77]Find out more about Dag Heward-Mills at:

Healing Jesus Campaign
Write to: evangelist@daghewardmills.org
Website: www.daghewardmills.org
Facebook: Dag Heward-Mills
Twitter: @EvangelistDag

ISBN: 978-1-64329-259-5

Contents

1. The Gifts and Calling of God are without Repentance 1

2. The Difference between Secular Work and Ministry Work 7

3. What it Means to Walk Worthy of Your Calling 13

4. Ten Types of Workers 28

5. The Ten Laws of Your Mission 34

6. How to be a Good Personal Assistant 40

7. The Laws of Placement 46

8. How Your Value Is Determined 51

9. How to Enjoy Your Work 66

10. How to Find Your Life's Work 74

11. Why Some People Do Not Prosper at Work 79

12. How to Have Favour with Your Boss 82

CHAPTER 1

The Gifts and Calling of God are without Repentance

The First Call

Now the word of the LORD came unto Jonah the son of Amittai, saying, Arise, go to Nineveh, that great city, and cry against it; for their wickedness is come up before me.

Jonah 1:1-2

The Second Call

And the word of the LORD came unto Jonah THE SECOND TIME, saying, Arise, go unto Nineveh, that great city, and preach unto it the preaching that I bid thee.

Jonah 3:1-2

God is a God of mercy! He will give you a second chance to obey Him. Jonah is an example of someone who had a second chance to hear and obey. Sometimes we have only one chance!

The God of a Second Chance

Perhaps, God has always wanted you to work in a church and that is why He created you. Perhaps you have been running away from God's call. But God is speaking to you again. God spoke to Jonah twice. In between the first and second calls, Jonah had many experiences. He experienced the storms of life and the prison of the whale's belly. Perhaps after many hard experiences, you are ready to listen to God.

Perhaps as you hold this book, God is giving you a second chance to work in His house. It is time to join the army for the last battle.

No Change in the Call

You will notice that the first call and the second call were identical. In both the first and the second calls, Jonah was sent to the same city (Nineveh) with exactly the same message. The gifts and calling of God are without repentance (Romans 11:29).

God does not change His mind with the passage of time. Even after you have experienced the pain of storms and whales; bellies, He can still use you. Ten years may have passed since God first began to call you. It is not too late to obey Him. I am glad I serve the God who never changes His mind.

Accepting the call of God is accepting to be made into something that you are not. Jesus offered to make Peter into what he was not - a fisher of men!

Coming into the ministry is not about making some great contribution to the kingdom of God. Nothing depends on you and nothing will be destroyed by you neglecting the ministry. We are all expendable and dispensable.

For we can do nothing against the truth, but for the truth.

2 Corinthians 13:8

This Scripture teaches us that there is nothing we can ever do that will go against the truth of God's Word. Our greatest mistakes will not hinder the truth of the Gospel. Greatly neglecting our call cannot change the course of God's triumphant army. It is our privilege to be called to this work. It is our honour to be involved. It is time to stop thinking that you are going to do something unusual for God.

Being in the ministry is a humbling experience in which you actually learn about God and receive mercy. Jesus told His disciples to follow Him and He would make them into something. In full-time ministry, you will be moulded into a vessel God can use.

And Jesus said unto them, Come ye after me, and I WILL MAKE you to become fishers of men.

Mark 1:17

In full-time ministry, you will be transformed by the renewing of your mind and by the numerous humbling experiences that await you. Full-time ministry is actually the beginning of a journey that brings you closer to God. It changes you and makes you a humble person. The very nature of this despised work and the interaction with other Christians in ministry will surely break you down and make you a better person! Also, the interaction with outsiders who do not understand what full-time ministry is about will drive you deeper into God.

What Full-Time Ministry Is Not

Being in full-time ministry is when Jesus makes you into "fishers of men". Being paid by the ministry does not necessarily make you a full-time minister.

Switching your source of salary from the bank to the church does not mean you are in full-time ministry. Full-time ministry is an all-encompassing step in which you follow the Lord absolutely.

Your following Him will mean many things, including some of the points listed below.

Full-time ministry is not as simple as switching jobs. It is a lifetime commitment. It will swallow your whole being and you will be transformed by the power of God.

Full-time ministry is not any of these:

- Full-time ministry is not a convenient job option.

- Full-time ministry is not an easier job option.

- Full-time ministry is not a retirement plan for the elderly.

- Full-time ministry is not an arrangement for redeployed workers.

- Full-time ministry is not a refuge for mothers of little children.

- Full-time ministry is not a last-minute death wish for people who have spent their better years doing other things.

- Full-time ministry is not a camouflaged business plan. Some people want to use full-time ministry to ensure a regular salary whilst they do their businesses on the side. Business is business and ministry is ministry!

- Full-time ministry is not an activity for people in between jobs.

- Full-time ministry is not a springboard for men with secular ambitions.

- Full-time ministry is not a poverty alleviation scheme. Sometimes it is financially better to work in the ministry.

- Full-time ministry is not the same as transferring your profession from the secular world to the church. The fact that you were an accountant in the world does not mean that you must be an accountant in the church.

- Full-time ministry is not just about switching your source of salary.

- Full-time ministry is not a vacation job. Full-time ministry is not something for students to do to whilst on holiday.

Delusions about Full-Time Ministry

There are common current state delusions that plague people in different circumstances. People in full-time ministry are not spared their share of delusions. Some of the delusions that afflict a full-time minister are:

1. Because I am in full-time ministry I am special.

2. Because I am in full-time ministry I will have a good salary.

3. Because I am in full-time ministry I have taken the highest spiritual step and there are no more spiritual steps to be taken.

4. Because I am in full-time ministry I am better than lay ministers.

5. Because I am in full-time ministry I will travel to foreign countries.

6. Because I am in full-time ministry I will have a big house.

7. Because I am in full-time ministry I will have a car.

8. Because I am in full-time ministry I will be rich.

9. Because I am in full-time ministry I have become spiritual.

10. Because I am in full-time ministry I will have a better marriage and a better family life.

11. Because I am in full-time ministry I will have more time to pray, worship and study the Word.

12. Because I am in full-time ministry God is very pleased with me.

13. Because I am in full-time ministry I am walking in love.

14. Because I am in full-time ministry my judgment will be easy.

15. Because I am in full-time ministry I am anointed and protected.

16. Because I am in full-time ministry my children will turn out very well.

17. Because I am in full-time ministry I will go to Heaven by all means.

18. Because I am in full-time ministry I am loyal.

None of the things listed above are necessarily true. They may be true, but many of them may not be true in your case. And they are definitely not things that will happen automatically. You must seek God in full-time ministry so that all His plans will come to pass.

CHAPTER 2

The Difference between Secular Work and Ministry Work

There Is a Difference

But they will become his slaves so that they may LEARN THE DIFFERENCE between My service and the service of the kingdoms of the countries.

2 Chronicles 12:8, NASB

Whena Rehoboam rebelled against God, the prophet sent him a chilling message. He told him he would show him the difference between working for God and working for the nations of the world.

There is a difference between working for God and working for the world. Amassing wealth in this fading world cannot be compared with the high calling of God.

To build an eternal city with real foundations is the highest privilege for mortal man. Most men spend their lives building temporary things which have no future. The average man is simply a builder of temporal sandcastles.

Who Is Pharaoh?

Pharaoh is a "type" of Satan. Egypt is a "type" of the world and Israel is a "type" of God's people. Pharaoh afflicted God's people with hard labour and made them build treasure cities. This clearly depicts secular work today.

Most of the time spent in the secular world is spent building the cities of this world. By the time we are dead and gone, we have only added more beautiful buildings to the skyline of this world's cities.

The work of this world is with much rigour, much tension and much sweat. We are made to work harder and harder without realizing that we are actually building the treasure cities of this world. New York City, Paris, London, Accra, Lagos and Nairobi were built with the sweat of hard-working human beings.

These human beings are dead and gone but the treasure cities remain. Their life's work may be summed up as a contribution to the development of the treasure cities of the world. Mind you, Satan said to Jesus when he showed Him the nations of this world:

All this power will I give thee, and the glory of them: for that is delivered unto me; and to whomsoever I will I give it.

Luke 4:6

This shows us that it is actually Satan who exercises power over the cities of this world. The devil is the god of this world (2 Corinthians 4:4). It is Satan who has given the sons of men much hard labour and guided them to build the cities of this world.

Christians simply join the army of builders and contribute their quota to build these treasure cities.

Now there arose up a new king over Egypt, which knew not Joseph.
And he said unto his people, Behold, the people of the children of Israel are more and mightier than we:
Come on, let us deal wisely with them; lest they multiply, and it come to pass, that, when there falleth out any war, they join also unto our enemies, and fight against us, and so get them up out of the land.
Therefore they did set over them taskmasters to afflict them with their burdens. And they built for Pharaoh treasure cities, Pithom and Raamses.
But the more they afflicted them, the more they multiplied and grew. And they were grieved because of the children of Israel.
And the Egyptians made the children of Israel to serve with rigour:

Exodus 1:8-13

Just as Pharaoh controlled Egypt, Satan controls the world and its cities. That is why the entropy and confusion of this world is increasing steadily to its climax.

When you work in the financial institutions, banks and other secular organizations of this world, you can be compared to the Israelites working for Pharaoh; there is much rigour, much tension and much sweat about building sandcastles.

Moses requested that the people of Israel be set free so that they could serve the Lord. Anyone desiring to come into full-time ministry finds himself requesting a departure from the world system. Full-time ministry is service to the Lord! It is like going away from Egypt and into the desert to sacrifice to the Lord and build Him a tabernacle!

God wants His people to spend their time building Him a tabernacle and worshipping Him.

Of course, escaping from the world system is not going to be easy. It was not easy for Moses and the children of Israel to leave Egypt. It was only through a determined struggle that the people of God finally escaped from Pharaoh.

Dear friend, it will not be easy for you to escape from secular work. If it happens it will be through much struggle.

Four Stages for Escape from Pharaoh

And it came to pass, when PHARAOH WOULD HARDLY LET US GO...

Exodus 13:15

Pharaoh was not pleased to let the children of Israel go free. There are four stages that every Christian may go through in order to break out into full-time ministry. You must recognize each of these situations when you are presented with them.

Stage 1: *Pharaoh does not want you to leave his employment.*

And Pharaoh said, Who is the Lord, that I should obey his voice to let Israel go? I know not the Lord, NEITHER WILL I LET ISRAEL GO.

Exodus 5:2

Pharaoh wants you to work for him until you are dead. He wants you to sweat and toil until you die. Satan knows that many people will never reach the retirement age. He deludes them into working towards an imaginary retirement which will never materialize.

Stage 2: *Pharaoh will allow you to serve God but wants you to remain with him.*

And Pharaoh called for Moses and for Aaron, and said, Go ye, sacrifice to your God IN THE LAND.

Exodus 8:25

In this next stage, Pharaoh yields to some pressure. He agrees that you should serve God but you must remain in Egypt. You must continue to build Pharaoh's pyramids. This form of service is politely called the lay ministry. Serving God, but well fastened to the world system of earning money!

Pharaoh will prescribe when you can go to church and when you cannot. Once you are in his land, you belong to him and he decides everything you do. He decides when you wake up and when you go to bed. He decides what you do everyday of the week. He leaves you with only Sundays to relax but sometimes he will take even that from you.

Why should Pharaoh tell you to serve God only on Sunday afternoons and Wednesday evenings? Why can't you serve God on Monday mornings as well? Why should Pharaoh control what I do on Tuesdays, Wednesdays, Thursdays and Fridays? When Moses led the people of Israel to the wilderness, they were free to serve the Lord exclusively.

This is the ultimate desire of God for every one of His children. Sadly though, very few ever get to this state of perfect liberation from Pharaoh and all that he represents.

Stage 3: *Pharaoh does not want you to go too far.*

And Pharaoh said, I will let you go, that ye may sacrifice to the LORD your God in the wilderness; ONLY YE SHALL NOT GO VERY FAR away: intreat for me.

Exodus 8:28

In stage three, you are warned not to go too far with God and the ministry. Many Christians side with Pharaoh at this stage.

Good and moral Christians will warn of the dangers of extremism. Today's church is full of "Mr Good" and "Mrs. Perfect" who are neither hot nor cold. It is a church of "mature," moral, never-do-wrong Christians who neither go too far nor too near! "Mr. Clean" is neither hot nor cold!

Something in between will do! When you suggest the idea of full-time ministry, they say you should not go too far.

Stage 4:   *Pharaoh does not want you to risk your finances in ministry.*

And Pharaoh called unto Moses, and said, Go ye, serve the Lord; ONLY LET YOUR FLOCKS AND YOUR HERDS BE STAYED: let your little ones also go with you.

Exodus 10:24

Today's lukewarm Christians want to serve God without risking anything. They fully agree with Pharaoh's suggestion about serving the Lord without risking their businesses or their earthly possessions.

The modern church, including the modern pastor, is amazed at the idea of professionals leaving their vocations for the ministry. What a glorious honour it is to receive an invitation of the Lord to build His tabernacle!

Yet, the voices of the ones who are neither hot nor cold drown the voice of the Spirit. They say, "Don't risk your life, don't risk the flocks, and don't risk your resources on a crazy adventure. Don't follow this crazy man."

Dear friend, there is no higher calling than to serve the King of Kings. Fight your way out of prison. Make it your life's ambition to follow the pillar of cloud and the pillar of fire. Make it your life's work to build His tabernacle rather than building the treasure cities of Pharaoh.

CHAPTER 3

What it Means to Walk Worthy of Your Calling

...walk in a manner worthy of the calling with which you have been called,

Ephesians 4:1, NASB

The Apostle warns us all to walk in a manner worthy of the calling. I became a medical doctor in 1989. I had been in medical school for seven long years. It was a strange feeling to suddenly be a "respected" medical doctor. I had been a student for so long.

For the last twenty-five years of my life, I had been treated as a "young" student. Now, I was a "prestigious" doctor. I couldn't do some of the things I did before. I had to live up to the new and esteemed image of a medical doctor.

So it is with ministry. God wants you to live up to your new vocation of full-time ministry. You must endeavour to accomplish all that God has desired for you.

Understand Why You Must Walk Worthy

1. You must walk worthy because it is a privilege to be chosen.

Therefore seeing we have this ministry, as WE HAVE RECEIVED MERCY, we faint not.
2 Corinthians 4:1

It is truly a privilege to be chosen by the Lord. To be saved is the highest privilege a human being could have. When I consider the millions of people who live and die, never knowing the Lord, I consider it my greatest blessing to be saved.

When I consider my friends and relatives who do not know the Lord, I am eternally grateful for my salvation. What more could I ask for? Yet there seems to be something higher that God is giving to some of us - a call to full-time ministry! This truly is the mercy of God. That is why you must walk worthy. To work for God is the opportunity very few people in this world will ever have.

2. You must walk worthy because you have a limited season of opportunity.

This is what applies to the Levites: from twenty-five years old and upward they shall enter to perform service in the work of the tent of meeting.

But at the age of fifty years they shall retire from service in the work and not work any more.

Numbers 8:24-25, NASB

From the Scripture above, a short period is allotted for the work of ministry. Some people delay unduly and lose their opportunity to work for God. It is a blessing if you responded to this call in time. It takes the grace of God to respond in time or even to respond at all!

If you find yourself working in a church, be thankful and behave yourself wisely because it is a privilege.

3. You must walk worthy because the grace of God has worked for you.

By the grace of God I am what I am...

1 Corinthians 15:10

It takes the grace of God to even hear the call. It takes the grace of God to respond appropriately to the call of God. Most human beings do not respond appropriately to the call. Jonah messed things up and had to be swallowed by a whale. Moses could not accept his call until Aaron was brought into the picture.

Many people stay away from ministry because they do not know what their calling is. Some simply do not have the opportunity to work in a church. Paul said, "I am what I am by the grace of God." How true that is!

Coming into full-time ministry can be very complicated. Parents and friends are likely to oppose the ministry. I struggled to enter full-time ministry. I tried business and other ventures. I tried to go to America to be close to a man of God so I could learn from him. None of these things worked out. When my father found out that I was not planning on becoming a specialist doctor, he warned me and told me I was on my own. Through the financial help of my sister I was able to launch out into full-time ministry.

Many people are also encumbered with debts and other burdens. These things effectively keep people out of full-time ministry. Very few people are able to actually respond to the call of ministry.

If therefore you have been able to enter into full-time ministry, walk worthy of it because it was the grace of God that brought you in.

4. **It is more natural to live the life of an unbeliever than to serve God.**

   So this I say, and affirm together with the Lord, that you WALK NO LONGER JUST AS THE GENTILES also walk, in the futility of their mind, being darkened in their understanding, excluded from the life of God because of the ignorance that is in them, because of the hardness of their heart;
   Ephesians 4:17-18, NASB

The life of an unbeliever (a Gentile) follows a fixed pattern. Paul described this fixed pattern of living in Ephesians 4:17. There are three main characteristics of a Gentile's (unbeliever) life:

a. To live as an unbeliever is to walk in the futility of your mind.

Generally speaking, the life of an unbeliever is spent on futile and empty pursuits. It is a life of never-ending quests and useless ventures. Unbelievers spend their days building sandcastles, which are soon to be washed away by the sea. Everyone in full-time ministry could have spent his life chasing useless projects and imaginary goals. Sadly, the futility of all that men do is not obvious to them.

The heaping up of money, bank accounts and earthly treasures come to nothing but it is not easy to see. Most people never ask themselves why they are alive and why they are doing the things they do.

One day, a bank manager came to my house and left a complimentary card with the security man. When I woke up, the security man gave me the business card. As I studied this card, the Spirit said to me, "This lady is the manager of a sandcastle."

I was surprised at this statement coming from the Holy Spirit. But as I pondered over it, I realized that it was very very true. The bank is nothing but a sandcastle of imaginary wealth. It will perish and pass away with all its glory. I would rather be a door attendant in the permanent house of the Lord Jesus than to be the manager of a sandcastle organization.

The thinking of the Gentile mind is towards futility. Anybody who points out this futility looks strange. People would look at you strangely for calling the manager of a prestigious banking institution the manager of a sandcastle. In the world system, useless things are placed on a pedestal. They are feared and revered by one and all. It takes a man of the Spirit to see through the futility and the uselessness of it all. Surely, only a man of the Spirit can see and agree with the ancient Wisdom of Solomon: "...vanity of vanities; all is vanity" (Ecclesiastes 1:2).

b. To live as an unbeliever is to be darkened in understanding.

The life of an unbeliever is lived out through his darkened (limited) understanding. Darkness imposes limitations on all activities. There are many things we cannot do in the night. Movement is restricted and most workplaces are closed. Nightfall and darkness therefore impose severe limitations on those experiencing it.

A Gentile, someone whose understanding is darkened, is therefore operating with a severely limited understanding. His thinking has been greatly reduced (darkened). He cannot see beyond this life.

Working in full-time ministry is only possible if limitations on your mind are lifted and you can see beyond this life. People in full-time ministry are seeing beyond this life. My eyes are fixed on eternal rewards.

I recently heard of how a very young executive of a billion dollar company died. It was sad because he was at the peak of his career. He had achieved many things older people could not achieve. However, he was struck with cancer and had to die sooner than he expected.

For whom shall be the things he had acquired? Where will they be stored? How long will they last? Will he be coming back to enjoy them? Will the people he left behind eat his millions while he is in the grave? Will his successors be wise or foolish? These are the questions someone with a darkened understanding is unable to answer. His mind is too limited to even think of these issues. These issues are too heavy for a darkened mind!

c. To live as an unbeliever is to be excluded from the life of God.

Unbelievers are excluded from the life of God. It is easy to exist on this earth without ever experiencing the life of God. Exclusion from the life of God is living without God's involvement and direction! You live by the uselessness of your own thinking.

You may create happiness in your myopic world but the absence of God in your life will lead to your eventual destruction.

Adam and Eve lived happily in the garden where God visited them. They had a job given to them by the Lord. After the incident with the tree of the knowledge of good and evil, they died and began to experience death. They were condemned to an existence of sweating and toiling for mere food. Their life was destroyed. They were no more living. They were existing and surviving to gather food for themselves. Life had lost its meaning because they were excluded from God.

Without the life of God, all your labour is to provide food, drink, clothing and shelter. With the life of God, you live for a higher purpose. You live to fulfil God's plan for your life. You live to obey His Word. That is the life of God!

The millionaires of this world do not know why they are alive. For whom do they labour? When will they get the chance to eat up all their treasures? Will they take these treasures away from this earth? What will happen to them when they die?

Exclusion from the life of God takes place because of ignorance of the Word. Born-again Christians must ensure they are not excluded from the life of God through ignorance. Constantly studying the Word of God will change you and bring you deeper into the life of God.

Throughout my years in ministry, I have learnt some things about handling God's privileges. Perhaps the most important thing to do in your privileged position is to walk worthily and carefully. God's grace must motivate you to walk worthily.

Don't Offer Strange Fire!

Live and conduct yourself carefully in this ministry. Nadab and Abihu are examples of priests who did not walk carefully in their calling. They died whilst walking in their calling of full-time ministry. They did not die because they were thieves or murderers. They died because they did not practise their ministry in the right way. They offered strange fire to the Lord. They did not walk worthy of their calling.

Now Nadab and Abihu, the sons of Aaron, took their respective firepans, and after putting fire in them, placed incense on it and offered strange fire before the LORD, which He had not commanded them.
AND FIRE CAME OUT FROM THE PRESENCE OF THE LORD AND CONSUMED THEM, and they

died before the LORD. Then Moses said to Aaron, "It is what the LORD spoke, saying, 'By those who come near Me I will be treated as holy, And before all the people I will be honored'." So Aaron, therefore, kept silent.

Leviticus 10:1-3, NASB

We want to study how to offer God the kind of service and sacrifice He loves. We want to practise full-time ministry in a way that pleases God.

There are many Scriptures that exhort us to walk worthy of our calling. I was surprised to find that walking worthily involves developing important spiritual virtues like humility and patience. God's idea of how to walk worthy is probably different from yours. Notice these three Scriptures that exhort us to walk worthily in the ministry.

Therefore I, the prisoner of the Lord, implore you to WALK IN A MANNER WORTHY OF THE CALLING with which you have been called, with all humility and gentleness, with patience, showing tolerance for one another in love, being diligent to preserve the unity of the Spirit in the bond of peace.

Ephesians 4:1-3, NASB

So that you will WALK IN A MANNER WORTHY OF THE LORD, to please Him in all respects, bearing fruit in every good work and increasing in the knowledge of God; strengthened with all power, according to His glorious might, for the attaining of all steadfastness and patience; joyously

Colossians 1:10-11, NASB

Therefore, SINCE WE HAVE THIS MINISTRY, as we received mercy, WE DO not lose heart, but we have renounced the things hidden because of shame, not walking in craftiness or adulterating the word of God, but by the manifestation of truth commending ourselves to every man's conscience in the sight of God.

2 Corinthians 4:1-2, NASB

Twenty Ways to Walk Worthy

1. Be humble in full-time ministry.

...walk in a manner worthy...with all humility...

Ephesians 4:1-2, NASB

The most important way of walking worthy is to walk in humility.

Recently, whilst writing a book, I had a revelation about a great ministry that had gone down from its former glory. The Lord showed me in a flash that those people had not walked in humility when their ministry grew. This church had publicly criticized other ministries and ridiculed ministers from their pulpit. At the peak of their ministry, they would ask people who came from other churches to stand up for cleansing (from the contamination of other ministries).

There are many ways to respond to God's promotion in ministry.

When the Lord gave Solomon the blessing of building a mega temple, he did not praise himself or think more highly of his achievements than he should. He actually demeaned his own achievements. He declared that the temple he had built was nothing. He knew that his great temple was simply a human attempt to do something for the Lord.

Notice the prayer of Solomon:

But will God indeed dwell on the earth? Behold, heaven and the highest heaven cannot contain You, how much less this house which I have built!

1 Kings 8:27, NASB

When you accomplish something for the Lord, you must see it in the right light. You have done nothing! God did not need you or me. It is His grace that makes it possible for us even to be around.

2.   Gentleness in full-time ministry

...walk in a manner worthy...with gentleness...

Ephesians 4:1-2, NASB

To be gentle means to do things gradually. When you are in full-time ministry you must do things gradually. If you try to achieve certain heights in a hurry, you will have disaster. There are new ministers who want to be on television and radio in the first part of their ministry. Others want to write books because everyone is writing a book.

When you are not gentle, you push others around and you become frustrated about your apparent lack of success in the ministry.

3.   Patience in full-time ministry

...walk in a manner worthy...with patience...

Ephesians 4:1-2, NASB

You must be patient in full-time ministry. You will not succeed overnight. Most of the casualties of full-time ministry were impatient. They could not wait to be bishops. They were not content with little things they were given to do. They wanted to hurry to the top. They drove faster and faster until there was a terrible accident.

4.   Tolerance for one another in full-time ministry

...walk in a manner worthy...showing tolerance for one another...

Ephesians 4:1-2, NASB

It is necessary to be tolerant of others in the church. Working in a church involves working with others. You need to accept others as you work with them. Just like any other workplace, the church is full of human beings.

As soon as there is strife in the church, the anointing of the Lord is hindered. Let nothing be done through strife (Philippians 2:3). Full-time ministry must not be practiced through strife. Quarrels in the ministry should be treated as emergencies. They should be dealt with and the atmosphere of love must be maintained.

5. Staying united in full-time ministry

...walk in a manner worthy...to preserve the unity of the Spirit...

Ephesians 4:1, 3 NASB

Staying united is very important to the Lord. Whatever you do in the church, do not create division. If you create divisions, you are not walking worthy of the privilege of ministry. There is one body and we will not allow anyone to divide us into groups based on tribe, nationality or any other idea.

6. Ensure peace in full-time ministry.

...walk in a manner worthy...to preserve...the bond of peace.

Ephesians 4:1, 3 NASB

Peace is essential for building. King Solomon was able to build many things because he had peace. Solomon's armies were used for building instead of fighting. Any ministry which fights within itself will not build much for God.

7. Please God in full-time ministry.

...walk in a manner worthy...to please Him...

Colossians 1:10, NASB

Surprisingly, not everybody in full-time ministry pleases the Lord. It is important to please God in whatever you do. Like Nadab and Abihu, God may be displeased with you even though you spend most of your time in the church. Endeavour to please God even in full-time ministry. For instance, I know of only one thing that causes a stir in Heaven - soul winning. When you win a soul, you make the Father happy. Soul winning is one of the many activities a full-time minister can pursue. I assure you, it is one thing that will please the Father.

8. Be fruitful in full-time ministry.

...walk in a manner worthy...bearing fruit...

Colossians 1:10, NASB

There are differences in employees. Some members of staff are very fruitful and contribute greatly to the efforts of the ministry. Others are more of a burden. Ensure that you are one of those whose presence is beneficial to the work of God. The fact that you are paid by the organization does not mean that you are fruitful.

9. Increase in the knowledge of God in full-time ministry.

...walk in a manner worthy...increasing in the knowledge of God;

Colossians 1:10

One interesting phenomenon is that some people actually backslide when they are in full-time ministry. They actually pray less and read less than when they were lay people. The fact that you work in a church does not mean that you will be automatically full of the Word. Endeavour to increase in the knowledge of God even as you serve God in full-time ministry.

10. Become stronger spiritually.

...walk in a manner worthy...strengthened...

Colossians 1:10-11, NASB

You must become stronger spiritually now that you are in full-time ministry. Pray more and wait on the Lord. God will bless you.

11. Be steadfast in full-time ministry.

...walk in a manner worthy...attaining...all steadfastness...

Colossians 1:10-11, NASB

You must be steady and unmovable in the ministry. Financial pressures and job offers must not be able to move you away from your calling. As you work in full-time ministry, you will attain steadfastness. Steadfastness is the ability to stay on course. Steadfastness is also the ability to come back to the course when you drift away. Do not drift from full-time ministry. There are many things to drift into. Business, education, relief work, social work, etc., are common roads that full-time ministers drift into.

12. Become happy in full-time ministry.

...walk in a manner worthy...joyously
Colossians 1:10-11, NASB

Full-time ministry is a joyful time. You must have a joyful attitude in ministry. Working in the ministry is better than working in the bank. Full-time ministry is better than working in the hospital. People who have tasted working for the Lord will not want to go back to the world.

13. Be thankful that you are in full-time ministry.

...walk in a manner worthy...giving thanks...
Colossians 1:10,12 NASB

Your heart must be full of thanks everyday for the great opportunity that God has given you to work for Him. If you are not thankful, you are probably in the wrong place. The more time you spend working in the ministry, the more thankful you should become.

14. Do not lose heart in full-time ministry.

...since we have this ministry...we do not lose heart
2 Corinthians 4:1-2, NASB

Ministry is not easy. There are many things that can discourage you. Much of what you do is hard work, with no one appreciating your efforts. You are working for the Lord and not for any man. It is when you look to people for appreciation that you become discouraged.

15. Renounce hidden things of dishonesty.

...since we have this ministry...we have renounced the things hidden because of shame...
2 Corinthians 4:1-2, NASB

Dishonest people cannot flourish in ministry. The reason is that the boss (God) has His eyes everywhere. Unlike other jobs where you can get away with stealing and other dishonest practices, you cannot steal from God.

There are people who think they have duped the Lord but no one can hoodwink the King of Kings.

16. Do not be crafty.

Since we have this ministry...not walking in craftiness
2 Corinthians 4:1-2, NASB

Craftiness speaks of being cleverly able to cut corners and get away with poor work. Unfortunately, this is not possible with Jehovah. Leave your crooked ways behind and let us work for the Lord without craftiness.

17. Do not adulterate the Word of God.

...since we have this ministry...not...adulterating the word of God...
2 Corinthians 4:1-2, NASB

The Word of God cannot be tampered with. Many people have tried to water down His precious Gospel. They have sought to re-present the Gospel as some kind of good advice for successful living. We cannot do anything that will destroy the truth of God's work. Do not change His Word; just preach it as it is.

18. Commend yourself to the conscience of men.

...since we have this ministry...commending ourselves to every man's conscience...
2 Corinthians 4:1-2, NASB

It is important to commend yourself to men's consciences. Often they will criticize you but in their hearts they respect what you are doing.

19. Commend yourself to men in God's sight.

...since we have this ministry...commending ourselves to every man's conscience in the sight of God.

2 Corinthians 4:1-2, NASB

All that we do must have approval in the sight of God. No human being or human institution can declare our work approved or disapproved. It is time to think only of what God says.

20. Make sure the Gospel is not hidden because of us.

And even if our gospel is veiled, it is veiled to those who are perishing, in whose case the god of this world has blinded the minds of the unbelieving so that they might not see the light of the gospel of the glory of Christ, who is the image of God.

2 Corinthians 4:3-4, NASB

Finally, the aim of full-time ministry is to ensure that the Gospel is known and heard in every corner of the world. How unfortunate it is that many people do not hear the Gospel.

All the efforts and money of the modern church must be directed to ensure that the Gospel is not hidden even from the remotest village. The Gospel must not be hidden from the poor. The way we operate the ministry must ensure that the Gospel is not hidden from anyone.

CHAPTER 4

Ten Types of Workers

1. Workers who are sons and daughters

But ye know the proof of him, that, AS A SON WITH THE FATHER, he hath served with me in the gospel.

Philippians 2:22

There are people who work in the ministry as sons and daughters of the ministry. Such people live and work as though they are in a family business. They do not have the usual employee attitude. They are more of family members. Also, such people do not have the usual "I am here for what I can get" attitude.

I find that many difficulties are eliminated by working with sons and daughters. You will probably enjoy working with your father more than with your boss!

In reality, not all workers in full-time ministry are sons or daughters of the ministry. Some are simply good people who want to work for God.

2. Workers who have the same spirit as the leader

I desired Titus, and with him I sent a brother. Did Titus make a gain of you? walked we not in THE SAME SPIRIT? walked we not in the same steps?

2 Corinthians 12:18

There are people who work in the ministry but have a different spirit from their leader. It is a blessing to find people who work with you with "the same spirit".

Paul was not in the ministry for financial gain and he found in Titus someone with the same spirit. You do not need to stay long in the ministry to find out that people work in the ministry for different reasons. What a blessing it is to find someone who will work with you in the ministry with the same spirit!

3. Workers who work for you because they owe their whole life to you

I Paul have written it with mine own hand, I will repay it: albeit I do not say to thee how thou OWEST UNTO ME EVEN THINE OWN SELF besides.

Philemon 1:19

There are people who work in the ministry out of a sense of gratitude and indebtedness to God. Such people are often grateful for their salvation and feel that they owe their lives to you.

If people really understood what their salvation was, they would spend the rest of their days in full-time service to God. Seventy years of working for God would not be able to pay for the blessing of salvation.

4. Workers who are prone to abandoning you

For DEMAS HATH FORSAKEN me, having loved this present world, and is departed unto Thessalonica; Crescens to Galatia, Titus unto Dalmatia.

2 Timothy 4:10

Every ministry has a "Demas". Demas is the minister or employee who abandons ship in the midst of the journey. Do not become the Demas of your church and ministry.

There are people who are given to you for life. God has called some of us to live and work together for the rest of our lives. There is a feeling of peace as you work with this permanent family.

Sadly, there is a type of full-time minister who will abandon you midstream. After being in the ministry for some time, I can often see the type of person who will suddenly resign from the ministry.

5. Workers who refresh you

The Lord give mercy unto the house of Onesiphorus; for HE OFT REFRESHED ME, and was not ashamed of my chain:

2 Timothy 1:16

The most refreshing people are those who are not ashamed of you. They love everything about you, including the unattractive parts. It is only the deepest kind of love that embraces everything; the good, the bad and the ugly.

Such people are not serving you for money. They are there because of a very personal love for the leader. I always sense when people have a personal love for me. I also sense when they know I am not perfect but they still love me.

Every minister has a shameful chain around him. Not everyone who works in the ministry has this personal and permanent love. May you have the spirit of Onesiphorus. May you bring refreshing to the man God has called you to.

6. Workers who are servants of the church.

I commend unto you Phebe our sister, which is A SERVANT OF THE CHURCH which is at Cenchrea:

Romans 16:1

There are people who bestow much service on the church in general. They are a blessing to many people. The impact of the servants of the church is seen best when they die. I have never forgotten the different people who have served me through the years.

Some have made themselves into errand boys and girls. They have served and helped in almost every imaginable capacity. I know that God will bless them on the Day of Judgement.

Although most church members' deaths would go unnoticed, the whole church feels the loss of the Phebes of the ministry. Phebe, without using the pulpit, touched the lives of many people.

7. Couples who are in full-time ministry together

Greet Priscilla and Aquila my helpers in Christ Jesus:

Romans 16:3

It is a special privilege for a man of God to have both husband and wife working together to help him. What a blessing it is for the whole family to work together in full-time ministry.

It is a special blessing for couples to both find a place in the house of God. Couples in ministry have a more synchronized lifestyle that may enhance their relationship.

Many full-time ministers take Mondays as their day off. However, in the secular world, Monday is the first and most important day of the week. This difference in schedules can separate couples who do not work together in the ministry.

In addition, a spouse who does not work in the ministry often despises the one in full-time ministry. They think their spouses are wasting their time by working for a church. They do not respect the ministry and therefore they do not respect people who work full-time in it.

These people also do not understand what could make someone busy in the church. Because the secular spouse despises full-time ministry he often sends the full-time spouse on domestic errands. Sadly, such people see the spouse in full-time ministry as unemployed.

There are also disadvantages of couples working in the same place, but the advantages outweigh the disadvantages.

8. Hard-working workers

Greet Mary, who bestowed MUCH LABOUR on us.

Romans 16:6

There are always the workhorses of ministry. Ministry involves a lot of hard work and there are always people who take on the burden of the work. They bestow much labour and exert much effort to accomplish ministry tasks.

This is what Paul meant when he spoke of Mary who worked so hard when he visited. God sees all the hard work that everyone puts into the ministry and He will reward it.

In His letter to the Ephesian church, the Lord made special mention of the labours and the hard work of the church. God notices hard work!

I know thy works, and thy labour, and thy patience, and how thou canst not bear them which are evil... And hast borne, and hast patience, and for my name's sake hast laboured, and hast not fainted.

Revelation 2:2-3

9. Workers who are women and cannot stop quarrelling

I beseech Euodias, and beseech Syntyche, that they be of the same mind in the Lord

Philippians 4:2

Women are most precious workers who love the Lord with all their heart and with all their feelings. One of the side effects of ladies working together is female bickering and quarrelling.

Paul found himself in the middle of female quarrelling and had to dedicate part of his church letter to solving a problem between two ladies.

Some of these quarrels and cold wars may be inevitable when women work together. God wants women to work for Him and they have a valuable contribution to make!

As we mature in the love of God, the Euodias-Syntyche syndrome will surely manifest! But the love of God will smoothen out all these things.

10. Full-time apostles

Salute Andronicus and Junia, my kinsmen, and my fellow prisoners, who are of note among the apostles, who also were in Christ before me.

Romans 16:7

The work of the apostle is to create something that did not exist. There are some workers who can make something out of nothing. You can send them on a mission and they will bulldoze their way through all obstacles, accomplishing and creating as they go along.

In every ministry, there are people whose contribution is of special note. After the apostle has built the church, every other ministry has something to do. Truly, the apostles are noteworthy among the team of full-time workers.

Beginning a ministry is very difficult. It takes determination, faith and resilience to pull through with a pioneering work. We must respect the grace of God that is upon apostles amongst us who are able to begin things that stand the test of time.

CHAPTER 5

The Ten Laws of Your Mission

Working in the ministry is working for Christ Jesus. He has given us guidelines for the accomplishment of His mission. When He commissioned His apostles, He said many things which were intended to guide them in full-time ministry. These instructions can be called the "Laws of the Mission" since they serve as a guide on how to behave during the mission. I want us to go through several of these Laws of the Mission.

1. The law of knowing your calling

For ye see your calling, brethren, how that not many wise men after the flesh, not many mighty, not many noble, are called:

1 Corinthians 1:26

It is important to know your particular calling. Most people do not know what their calling is. As you serve the Lord, you will see things which help reveal your particular call. The Bible teaches that you see and know things about your calling.

For ye see your calling, brethren, how that...

1 Corinthians 1:26

It is important to discover a lot about your calling and to know what it actually involves.

But go rather to the lost sheep of the house of Israel.

Matthew 10:6

The disciples were called specifically to the house of Israel. Their call was to Israel and not to the Gentiles. If Jesus had not specifically told them to go to the lost sheep of Israel, with time the apostles would have noticed that their calling was to Israel.

For instance, they could have recognized a stronger anointing and more success when they ministered to the lost sheep of Israel. Perhaps they would have recognized how nothing worked when they tried ministering to Gentiles and Samaritans! They would soon have seen their calling; how that not many Gentiles or Samaritans were included in their ministry.

That is how you discover your calling. You watch what works. You observe what the Lord does with you and with your life. Then you begin to see and understand your calling. If you think you will have explicit details about your calling in a voice thundering from Heaven, you will probably wait forever. You have to watch your calling and flow with what God is doing.

2. The law of concentration and perfection

These twelve Jesus sent forth, and commanded them, saying, Go not into the way of the Gentiles, and into any city of the Samaritans enter ye not:

Matthew 10:5

In this law, Jesus teaches us to concentrate on our particular area of calling. In full-time ministry, we will only find true fruitfulness when we stay within the domain assigned to us.

Jesus told the Apostles to avoid Gentiles and Samaritans and concentrate on the lost sheep of Israel. When you know your calling, it is your duty to concentrate your efforts on your area of calling. As you do this you will become a better minister. People will recognize your gift in that area. This so-called gift is actually the fruit of you concentrating to perfect your calling.

3. The law of trusting God for finances

Provide neither gold, nor silver, nor brass in your purses, Nor scrip for your journey, neither two coats, neither shoes, nor yet staves: for the workman is worthy of his meat.

Matthew 10:9-10

Full-time ministry is all about trusting God for finances. Full-time ministry is not an alternative to your secular employment. Neither is it a place to achieve your financial aspirations.

It is all about trusting God for everything. God will take care of you as you work for Him. I cannot overemphasize this reality of ministry. Ministry is not for money. Ministry is for the service of God.

Anyone who does this sacred work with the intention of using the ministry as a source of riches is likely to end up in trouble. As old-fashioned as it may sound, you are going to have to trust God to provide everything for you.

4. The law of flexibility

And if the house be worthy, let your peace come upon it: but if it be not worthy, let your peace return to you. And whosoever shall not receive you, nor hear your words, when ye depart out of that house or city, shake off the dust of your feet.

Matthew 10:13-14

In ministry, you must be flexible and allow God to lead you in several different directions. It is good to start out trusting Him, but you must continue to be pliable in His hands. You must not be fixated to any particular role.

Sometimes, when something is not working, it is a sign that you must change direction. The Lord sent the disciples into the different cities. Some of these missions were doomed to fail but Jesus still asked them to go. However, He also told them to pack and leave immediately if the mission did not work.

Be ready to change course. Leave all options open. Be flexible and flow until you find your life's work!

5. The law of "absolute disconnection" from those who do not receive us nor believe in us

And whosoever shall not receive you, nor hear your words, when ye depart out of that house or city, shake off the dust of your feet.

Matthew 10:14

Not everybody is going to believe in your calling. There is no need to struggle with people who have reservations about what you are doing. Make new friends and stay with like-minded people. Avoid people who mock you. Blessed is the man that does not hang around mockers and scoffers.

There are people who consider full-time ministry to be madness of the highest order. There are born-again, Spirit-filled Christians who think that working in a church is for the elderly or emotionally unstable. Becoming a missionary is seen as something for people without a successful career.

6. The law of "snake wisdom"

Behold, I send you forth as sheep in the midst of wolves: be ye therefore wise as serpents, and harmless as doves.

Matthew 10:16

This law speaks of the importance and wisdom of privacy, confidentiality, and secrecy in ministry. It is fatally deficient wisdom to expose all that you are and all that you have to everyone. Once you are in the ministry, never believe that the world loves or accepts you. Assume that you are disliked, disbelieved, disregarded and disrespected by the world, its journalists and its politicians. We have been sent forth as sheep in the midst of wolves.

7. The law of wariness of men

But beware of men: for they will deliver you up to the councils, and they will scourge you in their synagogues;
Matthew 10:17

"Beware of men" are the words of Jesus to His disciples. He did not even say we should beware of devils. More harm can come to a minister through men than you imagine. A minister who makes close friends of worldly politicians and journalists may be setting himself up for an unpleasant experience.

Pastors are simply not respected by worldly business people and bank managers. Many of these businessmen see ministers as crooks. They just humour us and put up with us because they have to and because we sometimes give them good business. Beware of people who do not love you! Beware of men!

8. The law of the free Gospel

...freely ye have received, freely give.
Matthew 10:8

The Gospel was brought to us at no charge. We must endeavour to give it back freely. In order to give freely there are many things full-time workers must be conscious of.

We must reduce the cost of running the ministry. The cost of equipment, electricity, buildings, etc. must be brought to a minimum if we are to make the Gospel free. Our salaries also must be as low as possible. Does the ministry take care of our needs or does the ministry spend its money supporting our lifestyles?

9. The law of avoiding internal fighting

And he called them unto him, and said unto them in parables, How can Satan cast out Satan?
Mark 3:23

We stand no chance if we fight each other internally. There are some common but secret fights that go on in many churches and ministries. In the secret places of ministry, pastors often fight against other pastors.

Another internal but secret fight that goes on in the ministry is the fight between husbands and wives.

Yet another internal battle goes on amongst women who are jealous of each other. These battles are real and sometimes very bloody. Do not be surprised if you find yourself embroiled in one of these fights. But the warning is stern. We stand no chance against the real enemy if we exert our energies against one another!

10. The law of rewards

There is a reward for the smallest job in full-time ministry. Do not be discouraged if the work you do looks insignificant. In Heaven, you will be rewarded for your faithfulness to what you were given! I do not know what job you do, but I am sure it is more noteworthy than serving a glass of water. Is it not encouraging to know that even serving a glass of water will be rewarded in Heaven?

> **And whosoever shall give to drink unto one of these little ones a cup of cold water only in the name of a disciple, verily I say unto you, he shall in no wise lose his reward.**
>
> **Matthew 10:42**

CHAPTER 6

How to be a Good Personal Assistant

...who had ability for serving in the king's court...
Daniel 1:4, NASB

A s you set out to serve God in the ministry you may find yourself serving a man of God. Actually, the ministry is not about working in an institution but about serving an anointed man of God. Serving in the ministry is very different from working in the bank.

Not everyone will have the opportunity to work directly for the anointed man of God. Maybe, one day, you will have a chance to minister to God's servant personally. There are some things that are important for every full-time worker to know about becoming a personal servant to the man of God.

1. Accept the personal choices of the man of God.

And he goeth up into a mountain, and calleth unto him WHOM HE WOULD: and they came unto him.

Mark 3:13

Jesus chose whom He would. It was His personal decision. It was His preference. No one could choose His disciples for Him. Every leader has a right to choose those he wants to be with him.

God has designed us to make choices. Obviously, the leader cannot have everyone close to him.

Do not be angry if you are not chosen. Some people will be privileged and chosen to serve in the "king's court". This is a special calling. Do not fight the leader's choices. The leader will like you if you like his choice and will reject you if you reject his choice.

2. Accept the values of the man of God.

Every leader has personal needs. It is sometimes difficult to understand the needs and idiosyncrasies of some leaders. Depending on the needs a leader has, certain things will be important to him. The ability of someone to satisfy any of the special needs of the leader makes a person very valuable. Sometimes the value a leader places on the helper who meets his special needs may seem disproportionate to the importance ascribed to the person. You may not understand why the leader fusses over someone until you find yourself in his shoes.

Hiring a special singer or an organist may not seem important to some. For instance, a good singer may be worth millions to a ministering prophet.

Similarly, things that do not look valuable to us may be very valuable to God. You may be the most valuable person to God because you do something that your heavenly Father really loves.

3. Accept the man of God's need for genuine friends.

Every king needs friends, every king wants friends and every king has friends! If you can be the friend of the leader, you will be valuable to him.

King David's friend was Hushai the Archite (2 Samuel 15:37) and King Solomon's friend was Zabud (1 Kings 4:5). Jesus' friends were Lazarus, Martha and Mary, her sister.

Now Jesus loved Martha, and her sister, and Lazarus.

John 11:5

Every leader is still a human being and as such needs people to talk to. He needs people he can be relaxed with.

You can't be serious all the time; saying the right things, always behaving like the United Nations Secretary General on a diplomatic mission!

You need people with whom you can be relaxed and who are at ease around you. Somehow, not everyone can be relaxed in the presence of a king.

Also, most people cannot comprehend that they can have a down-to-earth friendship and relationship with the king. More and more, I realize that not everyone can serve in the king's court!

Shadrach, Meshach and Abednego were people who had, amongst other things, the ability to serve in the king's court. They had the special grace to hang around the king's environs and to relate with all that went on there.

Youths in whom was no defect, who were good-looking, showing intelligence in every branch of

wisdom, endowed with understanding and discerning knowledge, and who had ABILITY FOR SERVING IN THE KING'S COURT...

Daniel 1:4, NASB

A wise king knows that he is often surrounded by liars, thieves, treacherous people, wicked men, accusers, fault- finders and many poor and hungry-eyed men, looking for what they can get!

Oh, how he wishes for a few moments of respite, where he can be relaxed without fear. Perhaps it is in this that the friend finds his highest value! Someone with whom the leader can be at ease!

4. Accept the humble duties of a personal assistant.

There are servants who meet the personal needs of the leader. These personal servants may be demeaned in the eyes of onlookers.

Joshua was a personal servant of Moses but he became the leader of Israel. Elisha was the personal servant of Elijah and he received a double portion of the anointing.

Becoming a personal servant may be your door to the anointing! Indeed it is a privilege to pour water on the hands of the man of God, because very few people will ever have the opportunity to do that.

Verily, verily, I say unto you, He that receiveth whomsoever I send receiveth me; and he that receiveth me receiveth him that sent me.

John 13:20

5. Accept the spiritual opportunities that come with personal service.

And he ordained twelve, that they should BE WITH HIM, and that he might send them forth to preach,

Mark 3:14

The Lord did not take on the disciples for any particular job. He took them on so that they would be with Him.

There are many people that I employ just so that they will be near me. After being around the anointing for some time, people are ready to be sent.

Personal servants thus go through two phases of ministry. The first phase is the *"be with me"* phase. The second phase is the *"sending out"* phase.

6. Understand the dangers of familiarity in personal service.

For neither did his brethren believe in him.

John 7:5

Personal servants can easily become familiar. Through familiarity, Jesus' own family did not believe in him.

When you see the human side of God's servant, you can be tempted to think you are not dealing with the power of God. Perhaps this is what happened to Judas. All personal servants must be careful of becoming another Judas. Beware of familiarity.

7. Avoid the dangers of being unspiritual around a spiritual person.

...Martha, Martha, thou art careful and troubled about many things: But one thing is needful: and MARY HATH CHOSEN THAT GOOD PART, which shall not be taken away from her.

Luke 10:41-42

When you are involved in personal service, make sure you get the "good part". The *good part* of personal ministry is not the physical advantage, but the spiritual treasure. Unfortunately, many people who work closely and personally with a man of God miss the spiritual treasures of close fellowship.

The book of John reveals the treasures experienced when Jesus interacted personally and privately with His disciples.

The things He said were not for public consumption. They would never be heard by the crowds but they would be heard by the few around Him.

Martha was very close to Jesus but Jesus was not happy with her spirituality. He would have preferred it if she was more interested in the Word of God. *Every personal servant must be careful of being unspiritual around a spiritual person.*

Jesus knew that the job of serving food would be taken away from Martha. But the spiritual treasures that Mary was receiving were eternal. It is interesting to note that Jesus was still friendly to Martha even though she was not interested in the Word. Jesus still liked her very much and He enjoyed her food.

The fact that the spiritual leader likes you does not mean that you will do well on the Day of Judgement.

This is a common delusion for those in the personal company of spiritual leaders. They have the greatest privilege to be close but are in great danger of being unaffected by the anointing and the Word.

8. Accept the opportunity to become part of a new family.

Christ's disciples were one big family. This family spirit often develops as several people work in the personal service of the apostle.

Jesus called the people who worked with Him, His "mother" and His "brothers". This must be the pattern for all followers of Christ. Create a family out of your full-time staff! Let them be your brothers, mothers and sisters.

> **And he answered them, saying, WHO IS MY MOTHER, OR MY BRETHREN? And he looked round about on them which sat about him, and said, Behold my mother and my brethren!**
> **For whosoever shall do the will of God, the same is my brother, and my sister, and mother.**
>
> **Mark 3:33-35**

A family spirit can be nurtured in every workplace. This family spirit is even more important for growth in the ministry.

CHAPTER 7

The Laws of Placement

Everybody wants to be at the top and everybody wants to have the best possible job. Somehow, everybody must be placed in the most suitable position. So how do we get to the best places and what is the reason for being put in certain positions?

There are spiritual laws that govern where you must be placed in the ministry. In this chapter I want you to look at some of these laws so that you will have the understanding and the humility that is necessary to function effectively.

1. The law of "those who came first"

> ...After me comes a Man who has a higher rank than I, for He existed before me.
>
> John 1:30, NASB

This law teaches that those who come first are senior to those who come later. John the Baptist indicated that he had a senior in the ministry - Jesus Christ. He explained that Jesus was there before he was. In a spiritual sense, Jesus existed before John the Baptist. That is why Jesus was greater than he was.

2. The law of personal preference

This is another law that determines where you will be placed in the ministry. The "law of personal preference" can override the law of "those who came first". Generally speaking, the law of "who came first" usually applies.

Sometimes, someone who is a late entrant may be given a higher rank. This is because there may be other factors that necessitate a newcomer having a higher rank.

John came onto the ministry scene before Jesus. Yet Jesus was given a higher rank than him.

> **After me comes a Man who has a higher rank than I, for He existed before me.**
> **John 1:30, NASB**

Other Scriptures testify to the reality that God has a personal choice and He exercises it as He wills. God's election can override the law of "who came first".

> **For the children being not yet born, neither having done any good or evil, that the purpose of God according to election might stand, not of works, but of him that calleth. It was said unto her, The elder shall serve the younger. As it is written, Jacob have I loved, but Esau have I hated. What shall we say then? Is there unrighteousness with God? God forbid. For he saith to Moses, I will have mercy on whom I will have mercy, and I will have compassion on whom I will have compassion. So then it is not of him that willeth, nor of him that runneth, but of God that sheweth mercy.**
> **Romans 9:11-16**

3. The law of militarized work

> **No man that warreth entangleth himself with the affairs of this life...**
> **2 Timothy 2:4**

In full-time ministry, you cannot determine where you will be placed or where you will live. This is the reason why there are no guarantees and no securities in full-time ministry. The law of militarized work tells us that you can be sent anywhere at any time.

When you work in a militarized environment expect changes at any time. When you are in the army, you can be sent to your death at any time. Militarized work has no working hours. Militarized work is hard and full of risks. Many people die doing militarized work. You must have a militarized attitude in the ministry. Be ready to be sent anywhere or to be placed anywhere. Be ready to die for the cause when you are called upon.

4. The law of spiritual intimacy in ministry

Seemeth it but a small thing unto you, that the God of Israel hath separated you from the congregation of Israel, to bring you near to himself to do the service of the tabernacle of the LORD, and to stand before the congregation to minister unto them?

Numbers 16:9

The most important place for you is to be close to the Lord. Instead of seeking to be placed in seemingly prestigious positions, seek to be placed close to the Lord. Whether you are on the top floor or underground, aim to be close to the Lord.

Get this! Full-time ministry is intended to bring you close to the Lord; to make you an intimate friend of Jesus! God's intention for you in full-time ministry is to bring you close to Himself.

Notice what Moses told Korah. He pointed out that Korah had been brought near to do the service.

Spirituality and intimacy are choices you must make for yourself in full-time ministry.

5. The law of the candlestick position

This law teaches that love and intimacy will guarantee your position in the presence of the Lord. Everyone has a candlestick and your candlestick will be moved from where it is if you depart from love and intimacy with the Lord!

Hard work is no substitute for love and intimacy. God wants people to come close to Him. If we seek Him, we will find Him. In the book of Revelation, there was a church that worked harder than any other did. However, the Lord was not pleased with them. Hard work is not a substitute for a loving and intimate relationship. On two different occasions the Lord said to the church,

I know your labor." He knew they were a hard-working group.

He said to them:

I know thy works, and thy labour, and thy patience, and how thou canst not bear them which are evil: and thou hast tried them which say they are apostles, and are not, and hast found them liars:

And hast borne, and hast patience, and for my name's sake hast laboured, and hast not fainted. Nevertheless I have somewhat against thee, because thou hast left thy first love.

Revelation 2:2-4

They were indeed a labouring and toiling church but they were not intimate with the Lord. Because of this, they were in danger of being removed from their position. He warned them, "I will come and remove your candlestick out of its place."

6. The law of increasing goods

When goods increase, they are increased that eat them: and what good is there to the owners thereof, saving the beholding of them with their eyes?

Ecclesiastes 5:11

This law teaches that no matter where you are placed or what you earn, there will be things to swallow up your earnings.

Many workers are deluded into thinking that if they had a better position and earned more money they would be better off. But this is simply not the case.

As money increases, there are more things to do with the money. It is this delusion that drives people to attain certain positions. It is this delusion that makes workers dissatisfied with where they are placed.

Discover the secret of contentment. Believe that God rules in your affairs. You can be blessed in every position and in every circumstance.

CHAPTER 8

How Your Value Is Determined

etermining the value of anything is not easy. People go to the university for years to study "valuation". What is the value of a house? What is the value of a car? What is the value of a person? What is the value of a person to God? Obviously, the values of things change from person to person. Someone may value a diamond whilst another may kick it away as a worthless stone.

When you work for the Lord, you must seek to increase your value! You must understand what makes you valuable and do those things. You must understand what valuable thing God has placed in you and develop it.

Several things determine your value. Different people value different things. It is important to know some of the different things that increase or decrease your *personal* value.

How to Increase Your Value

1. Your value increases when you can be sent.

   ...Here am I; send me.

   Isaiah 6:8

Not everyone is sendable. A person being sent on a mission must have the special ability to be faithful without varying the message. Most people who are sent on a mission become sympathetic to the people they are sent to and modify their mission and their message!

If you look closely at the church today, you will find a modified message with a modified mission. I once sent somebody on a very simple mission. After a while, I realized that the person had become sympathetic to the group I had sent him to. This individual fell in love with the group and wanted me to support them financially. He constantly referred to the needs of the group rather than the message I had sent him with.

Once, without my knowledge, this person pledged my financial support to things I had not intended to do. After a while, I realized that I was sending the wrong person. My messenger had become sympathetic to the people he had been sent to. O how valuable it is to have someone you can send!

Someone who will not change the message! Someone whose heart will not change with time! Someone who will stay with the mission. Thank God for those who can stay with the message no matter how hard or ridiculous it sounds.

2. Your value increases when you can bring projects to a close.

To the inexperienced, this point may seem even frivolous. But I have employed different people, assigned them to various projects, and found them unable to conclude just the final little part.

Some people are able to start projects and carry them for a good distance. Amazingly, they are not able to conclude on their project even though they have come ninety per cent of the way. The last ten per cent of every project is a crucial final piece.

Hope deferred makes the heart sick; when the hope of accomplished tasks is dashed repeatedly, the heart of the leader is sickened.

A beautiful car, without one of its tyres, is the same as not having a car because a car with three tyres cannot be driven. Many people do not realize that one little uncompleted segment neutralizes everything else.

Jesus is the author and finisher of our faith. Some people are authors of things but not finishers. Your value greatly multiplies when you can finish what you have begun.

Every task has a whole lot of problems that will prevent its conclusion. Some people who are sent are unable to find solutions to these problems. They simply report back with their list of insurmountable problems.

However, the finisher will break through the barriers and overcome every obstacle. Such people are truly valuable. They just come home with a list of victories. They tell you how they overcame the different obstacles they encountered.

3. Your value increases when you can accomplish tasks with speed.

It is a pleasure to have a fast and reliable worker. I have had workers who accomplish tasks at different speeds. I prefer to work with people who bring projects to a close quickly. In fact, the value of someone who can rapidly conclude projects is very high.

I place a high premium on speed because delays are expensive and often lead to the cancellation of the original vision.

4. Your value increases with your ability to solve diverse problems.

There are people who can solve diverse problems and bulldoze their way through obstacles. I have people on my staff like that. They can deal with all kinds of people and solve all kinds of problems.

Whether the issues are private or public, they are able to sort them out. They can deal with difficult people, manage crises, help with personal matters and defeat the enemy. Such people are very valuable because life is full of diverse problems. Problems do not come in departments or under any particular headings. You need people who can solve problems no matter the category they fall into.

5. Your value is greater if you are involved in building a foundation.

You are those who have stood by Me in My trials; and just as My Father has granted Me a kingdom, I grant you that you may eat and drink at My table in My kingdom, and you will sit on thrones judging the twelve tribes of Israel.

Luke 22:28-30, NASB

The foundation of a building is the most difficult part to build. There are always some people who help to set things up. The contribution of such people is priceless. These people must never be forgotten. They are to be treasured and valued above those who come later. Anyone who wishes to set them aside does not understand what he is doing.

Jesus Himself promised His disciples that He would remember them especially because they had been with Him during the most trying times of His ministry.

Foundation builders suffer things that future workers will never experience. They experience the greatest pressures of the ministry. There are pastors who can build large churches but cannot actually begin one. Do not shy away from starting things. It may be your great opportunity to become valuable.

6. Your value increases with your ability to keep secrets.

No king would like to have a blabbermouth by his side. Many confidential things go on in the king's palace. Keeping things private and confidential may be one of the most important things to do. Anyone who works in the office of leadership must learn the importance of privacy and secrecy. Unfortunately, some people do not have the ability to work without talking about what they do.

Working in banks requires lots of secrecy because you deal with people's private wealth; one who cannot keep official information out of his domestic chatter will be unsuitable for such a job. Upon employment, banks will make you sign the oath of secrecy.

Working in a pastor's office may involve listening to private counselling sessions. Working in a doctor's office may also involve hearing and seeing people's personal problems. These private matters are nobody's business and should not be broadcast to the world. No one would like the whole world to know his personal problems.

Your value increases when you prove that you are capable of handling the responsibility of secrets. Some people will be employed simply because they do not have many friends! Some people will get certain jobs because they do not talk much with anyone about anything!

For this kind of job, you will have to avoid people who talk too much and have too many friends!

These "talkative" people will become valuable for the office party and other social gatherings where they will bring everything to life. Please understand what makes you valuable.

7. Your value increases when you are "good" company.

And he ordained twelve, THAT THEY SHOULD BE WITH HIM.

Mark 3:14

Jesus ordained twelve disciples simply so they would be with Him. He chose them to be in His company until He finished His ministry.

Not everybody can work comfortably with the boss. To work directly with the boss requires varied skills. The commander requires people who can engage in interesting and meaningful conversation. Some people just have nothing to say and therefore are not good company.

The Silent Hungry Look

Quiet people can be intolerable for a wise leader, as he has to constantly pry into their minds to find out what they are thinking.

His wisdom will cause him to search out hidden thoughts in case there are evolving plots against his life.

When I am with "quiet" people I always ask, "What do you think?" "How is your mind working? Is it a good idea?" I want to know what people around me are thinking.

Julius Caesar commented on Cassius, a worker in his court.

He said, "Yon Cassius has a lean and hungry look. He thinks too much: such men are dangerous."

Cassius was one of the conspirators who murdered Caesar. Long before the assassination, Caesar mistrusted Cassius because of the silent, hungry look on his face.

The Empty Look

Others only enjoy talking about light and frivolous matters, which may not interest the leader. Leaders are not light-hearted men of straw. They are serious people who have serious issues to deal with.

Rulers have many issues to juggle with and value people who are full of good counsel and wisdom. Leadership is a very lonely job with few who understand the real issues and challenges at hand. Many people simply see the leader as a superman who knows everything and who is always right. Such an attitude will not go well with a leader who wants the input of those around him. He therefore needs people who think and analyze issues in a certain way.

The Suspicious Look

A leader is someone who fights many battles. He does not need a cabinet member who is suspicious and opposed to all he does. This only transfers the battle from outside to within. Why should you employ someone to oppose and resist you?

Leaders also need people who think in a certain way. Paul said of Timothy,

> **...I have no man likeminded, who will naturally care for your state.**
>
> **Philippians 2:20**

King David had Hushai as his friend and King Solomon had Zabud as a friend. These friends were good company, good fellowship and gave good counsel.

The Creative Look

Creativity is the nature of God. People who are innovative and come up with good ideas when they are needed are also very valuable company.

Another important and valuable trait is the ability to meet the personal needs of the leader. Not everyone can work comfortably in the personal service of the king. Daniel and his three friends had the ability to serve in the king's court. This, too, is an important skill.

> **...bring in some of the sons of Israel...who had ability for serving in the king's court...they were to enter the king's personal service.**
>
> **Daniel 1:3-5, NASB**

8. Your value increases when you can relate well with outsiders.

There are people who can relate easily with the outside world. However, not all workers are up to this role.

To effectively relate with outsiders, you need to develop the art of diplomacy. You must understand protocol. Not everyone is skilled in diplomacy. Some people are simply unrefined and unrefinable!

Your dressing may have to be modified if you are to appear in public. Your speech will have to be appropriate and polished for the occasion. Some people simply do not have the background that enables them to function in this role.

Some people are unable to communicate with the public without offending people. Some simply do not have the patience or the ability to be a public relations person. A person who knows how to serve in the public eye is therefore valuable.

9. Having a specialized ability increases your value.

When you have some unusual talent, you become valuable. For instance, your ability to speak an unusual language can increase your value greatly. You must find a place where your particular ability is valued. There are people whose ability to sing has earned them special jobs in special places.

Not everyone has the ability to be a world-class singer. Some people have the ability to type with speed and accuracy. Such things give unusual value to a person. When I began to write books, I discovered how few people really know how to type with speed and accuracy.

The ability to host people and cater for them is also a special skill. Not every woman cares for people in a way that makes them feel at home. Some women actually drive people away with their unfriendly and expressionless faces. Some people do not even bother to learn what to do to make a particular person comfortable. Such motherly hosts are specially endowed and are of great value to churches that host guests frequently.

The ability to be a good public speaker or presenter is a special skill that can increase your value. Such a person may be invaluable for public relations and improving the corporate image of the organization.

Special computer skills and technical abilities can also make a person valuable. Discover what special ability you have and exploit it to the fullest. Let your gift make room for you and take you to the highest place!

10. You are valuable when you save the organization money.

There are people who have the ability to help save money. They negotiate on behalf of the organization as though they were negotiating for their own lives. Such people save lots of money for the ministry through their bargaining skills. People who make purchases and payments for the ministry are often not concerned about how much everything costs. But there are some who care and try to get the best deal every time. Such people are priceless treasures to an organization!

Other people view the opportunity to make a purchase on behalf of the organization as a chance to make some money for themselves. These are dangerous people who slowly undermine the ministry.

Paul said,

For I have no man likeminded, who will naturally care for your state.

Philippians 2:20

11. Your value greatly increases when you can work without supervision.

Supervising people can be one of the most tiresome jobs. Having to constantly monitor what someone is doing is wearisome, to say the least. What a joy it is to have someone who can work with little or no supervision. Just give him the job and he will come back with the results. When you have to chase a person, giving a hundred reminders and promptings about the same thing, you may just want to do the job yourself!

Unfortunately, most people need supervision and cannot be trusted to work on their own. Become someone who works without supervision!

12. Loyalty makes a person valuable.

Loyalty is more important than any qualification or skill I know. Any leader who does not value loyalty will live to discover the pain of treachery. A loyal person is far more valuable than an educated but disloyal person. When an employer does not know the value of loyalty, he often chooses people who are impressive but intrinsically disloyal.

After a while, these impressive people turn out to be painful choices. I have watched as ministers set aside faithful people and choose exciting people who have no loyalty. These people have not learnt about the great value of loyalty.

With the passage of time, most people will prefer a loyal person to any other. Every worker has to choose between his loyalty to the boss and his loyalty to the rest of the workers.

I once told a new employee, "You will either be liked by me or by the people. It's your choice." His value to me would rise greatly if he was loyal to me rather than to the rest of the staff.

13. Good organizers and managers are valuable.

Some people are able to gather people around and make them do their jobs. Others are simply unable to control anyone. I once found out that one of my newly appointed managers was unable to control the janitor. I realized that I had chosen the wrong person to be a manager.

Someone who is incapable of controlling drivers, cleaners and housemaids will not be able to control more educated and confident people. Your value goes up when you are able to control difficult people.

14. You are valuable when you are a contented person.

Satisfied people are a joy to have around.

Better is an handful with quietness...
Ecclesiastes 4:6

Moses had the difficulty of leading a discontented and grumbling crowd. Such people cannot be satisfied by anything. Good relationships are not built on money. No amount of money can make a person happy. Discontented people want more and more but they are never satisfied!

A worker who is happy with the little you can give is truly a valuable person. One discontented person can poison the entire workforce. Such people love to be part of unions, strikes and disruptions of work.

Such things are not needed in the church! Get rid of discontented people. Send them off to get a better job where they will be happier. It is not worth having them around.

15. Your value increases when you can learn anything required.

You may be required to produce television programs. If you are rigid and unprepared to learn completely new things, you will be limited in your value.

People who are prepared to learn new things are valuable! You may be required to run an orphanage or a radio station. Are you prepared to learn a completely new skill? I have watched as lawyers have learnt the art of construction and doctors have learnt how to run bookshops and schools. Their value increased because they were prepared to acquire new skills.

16. Long-standing workers are valuable.

Time speaks! Someone who has been around for years has a value that "Johnny-just-come" does not have! Years of stability and faithful service definitely confer value on every employee. Time tells whether a person is faithful or not!

Time tells whether a person is a liar or not. Time tells whether a person is a thief or not. Time tells whether a person is morally upright or not. The long years spent together assure us that we can depend on you.

17. Spirituality makes you valuable.

Spiritual people are valuable. Every church should endeavour to employ spiritual people. Sometimes spiritual people do not have certain qualities or abilities but their spirituality gives them great value in the ministry setting.

Unfortunately, some churches end up employing all sorts of unspiritual people; even unbelievers. They do this in order to fill some vacancies.

But it is often better not to have anyone, than to have a carnal person working in the church. Someone who has not been spiritual is not likely to become spiritual when he is in full-time ministry.

Gradually, a little leaven leavens the whole lump. Unspiritual and unsaved people gradually dilute the intensity of the zeal and anointing of any ministry. Soon you may have a full-time ministry staff of pseudo-Christians.

Wrong decisions will soon be taken because of the influence of carnal people. Full-time ministry is a place for zealous people who are on fire for Jesus. The Lord said to the Laodecian church, "I wish you were hot." God wants us to be hot and not lukewarm. Lukewarmness is a deadly enemy that destroys every true church.

18. Anointed people are valuable.

An anointed person is a special person with the grace of God operating in his life. Such people have great value because the grace and wisdom of God makes them operate above human ability. It is a joy to watch anointed people as they operate in the gift of God. They are special, they are different and they are wise!

> **The Spirit of the LORD will rest on Him, the spirit of wisdom and understanding, the spirit of counsel and strength, the spirit of knowledge and the fear of the LORD.**
> **And He will delight in the fear of the LORD, and He will not judge by what His eyes see, Nor make a decision by what His ears hear;**
> **Isaiah 11:2-3, NASB**

This is the wisdom that comes through the anointing. May you be an anointed worker!

19. Experienced people are valuable.

Experienced people have an uncanny knowledge of the future. Most things actually work out the way experienced people envisage.

Many things do not happen the way you would expect. There is some special knowledge that comes only through experience. People with experience often turn the tide in a battle. A person's value increases greatly because he is experienced. Do not shy away from things that make you experienced. The more experience you have, the more valuable you become.

20. Morality makes you valuable.

Moral and upright people are especially valuable as you can count on them to do the right thing behind closed doors. Joseph had the opportunity to sleep with his boss' wife but he did not. He could be trusted in very tempting circumstances. Such people are truly valuable.

The presence of one lecherous person (someone who is unduly interested in sex) can spoil the work of many years and end the employment of everyone else.

The higher you go in ministry the deeper your safety pegs must be. When you get to the eighth floor and you lean on the balcony, you would not want to discover that it is made of cardboard! The higher you go, the more the need for stronger character.

21. Working with excellence increases your value.

Sloppy workers who deliver shoddy work are a pain to most employers. They need extra supervision and are stressful to have around. What a joy it is to have someone who delivers a quality job every time! Such people are valuable and it is worth paying the price to have their services.

22. Your choleric personality makes you valuable.

Your choleric personality will make you valuable in difficult projects that need a driving force. This is the personality that will make you valuable in building up something from scratch. Choleric people are usually the best leaders but not very good assistants.

23. Your phlegmatic personality makes you valuable.

If God made you a phlegmatic, you will have special abilities, which no one else has. Phlegmatic people are stable workers and able to carry out monotonous jobs. There are many important jobs, which must go on in spite of their repetitiveness.

Where would we be without teachers and lecturers who stick to their jobs for years? These precious and steady trainers produce the high achievers and skilled workers of tomorrow. Phlegmatic workers are usually valuable because they are good assistants.

24. Your melancholic personality makes you valuable.

Melancholic people are usually very gifted and very organized. They are usually thoughtful, contented and deeply sacrificial. Melancholic people became the great missionaries of the past. These people are often quiet and can work where privacy and secrecy is required.

If God has made you a melancholic, you will be useful for many things in the office environment. You will keep things organized and private. You will have the ability to bring order and good management into places which are often disorganized.

25. Your sanguine personality makes you valuable.

If you are a sanguine, you will not be useful for things which require much organization. The scatter-brained and disorganized sanguine is of no use with sensitive documents. However, without a sanguine, your office will be a sad place! It will be lifeless because the life and excitement of the team is often created by the valuable sanguine. This is where a sanguine is most helpful.

If you put a melancholic in an office which a sanguine should occupy, people will leave because of the silent, stern and unfriendly melancholic.

I value the sanguine people in my office. They have no replacement. All the melancholics and cholerics put together cannot make the contribution of one sanguine.

CHAPTER 9

How to Enjoy Your Work

It is important to enjoy your work since that is what you will spend most of your time doing - working. Most people do not enjoy work and look forward to the slightest chance to escape.

It is therefore one of the greatest blessings to be given the kind of work that makes use of your God-given qualities.

Work then becomes like play, leisure and pleasure! No longer will you spend your working days longing for a vacation. No longer will you spend your working hours glancing at the clock and wondering why closing time is so far away.

It takes the God-kind of wisdom to enjoy work. You need to apply heavenly wisdom to what you are doing, otherwise you will end up depressed and wondering what life is about.

Even king Solomon, the richest and wisest man that ever lived, found life to be a vexation of spirit. He condemned his working experience on the earth and called it vanity. He spoke of the toil he had undertaken and the uselessness of it all. He considered the future and wondered what would happen to all the things he had built.

He thought to himself, "What if the person who comes after me destroys everything?"

Yea, I hated all my labour which I had taken under the sun: because I should leave it unto the man that shall be after me. And who knoweth whether he shall be a wise man or a fool? yet shall he have rule over all my labour wherein I have laboured, and wherein I have shewed myself wise under the sun. This is also vanity.

Ecclesiastes 2:18-19

As his melancholic thoughts deepened, he could only utter the words, "Vanity of vanities. All is vanity." Indeed, the one who succeeded him was a fool.

The son of the wisest man who ever lived (Rehoboam), indeed demonstrated great folly at his very first cabinet meeting. His very first decision split the kingdom up. The son of the wise man was now left with one tribe out of twelve to govern.

What a drastic reduction of the kingdom that his father had ruled! To make matters worse, he was unable to keep all the gold vessels that King Solomon had heaped up in the temple. Rehoboam replaced the golden vessels with brass - a poor substitute indeed! Solomon's son was a pale reflection of his father.

Such is the futility of all our life's work. It is vanity. Perhaps most working people have not reflected on these realities. If they do they would not find much meaning in what they are doing. This is the difference between secular work and full-time ministry.

When a Christian works for the Lord in full-time ministry, it is still important to apply a certain kind of wisdom.

This wisdom will make you enjoy your work and live joyfully under the sun. The term "under the sun" is used frequently in the book of Ecclesiastes. This phrase speaks of the life we live "under the sun" or the life we live on this earth. Solomon gave us words of wisdom that can dramatically improve life "under the sun".

However, most of the wisdom for life "under the sun" does not give guidance for the life hereafter.

If you fail to apply this wisdom "under the sun" you will probably hate your life in the end. You will find life and work a futile experience. Why would the Queen of Scotland say as she died, "Shame on life"? She sounded just like Solomon.

> **Therefore I hated life; because the work that is wrought under the sun is grievous unto me: for all is vanity and vexation of spirit.**
>
> Ecclesiastes 2:17

Wisdom for Enjoying Your Work

1. Enjoy your work by eating and drinking while you work.

The phrase "eat and drink" refers to having your basic needs met as you work. Eating good food and living well is wisdom that will make you enjoy working.

Some people save up for a good retirement but never reach that age.

> **Then I commended mirth, because a man hath no better thing under the sun, than to eat, and to drink, and to be merry: for that shall abide with him of his labour the days of his life, which God giveth him under the sun.**
>
> Ecclesiastes 8:15

It is time to enjoy your food and drink. Eat what you actually enjoy and drink to your fill. Bring out the best plates in the house and use the nicest glasses. Don't save them up for visitors any more. You are as good as any visitor!

> **Behold that which I have seen: it is good and comely for one to eat and to drink, and to enjoy the good of all**

his labour that he taketh under the sun all the days of his life, which God giveth him: for it is his portion.

Ecclesiastes 5:18

2. Be happy and joyful at work.

It is important to be joyful and happy whilst working. You will spend most of your lifetime working. You must enjoy the company of those you work with. You must be able to laugh, holler, and have a good time. If you do this, you will love going to work.

You will actually miss being at work because you will miss the good company and the good fun of it all. Home may even seem boring to you when you are joyful at work.

Then I commended mirth, because a man hath no better thing under the sun, than to eat, and to drink, and to be merry: for that shall abide with him of his labour the days of his life, which God giveth him under the sun.

Ecclesiastes 8:15

Fight till you work in the right environment and with the right people.

3. Accept your lot.

Then I realised that it is good and proper for a man to eat and drink, and to find satisfaction in his toilsome labour under the sun during the few days of life God has given him-- for THIS IS HIS LOT.

Moreover, when God gives any man wealth and possessions, and enables him to enjoy them, TO ACCEPT HIS LOT and be happy in his work-- this is a gift of God.

Ecclesiastes 5:18-19, NIV

Accept what God has given you. God has not given you everything. There are things we all wish we had but everyone must accept his lot. If you do not have a husband and spend all your life fighting to get one, you will probably become bitter and frustrated. If you do not have a child and spend the better part of your adult life trying to have one, you are likely to experience many disappointments.

As long as you do not accept your lot, you will have a life of unwinnable battles and humiliating defeats. "Accept your lot" is the wisdom of God for a happy life under the sun.

4. Enjoy work by living joyfully with your spouse.

LIVE JOYFULLY WITH THE WIFE whom thou lovest all the days of the life of thy vanity, which he hath given thee under the sun, all the days of thy vanity: FOR THAT IS THY PORTION IN THIS LIFE, and in thy labour which thou takest under the sun.

Ecclesiastes 9:9

One of the ways to enjoy your work is to live happily with your spouse. Anyone who has been married knows that marital conflict is a painful and discomfiting experience. It discolours everything and releases shadows of depression into your entire life. Indeed marital harmony is one of the rewards and blessings a person could have.

Many millionaires live alone and estranged from their wives. Their homes are filled with empty rooms and unused swimming pools. There are no shouts of joy and no peals of laughter from these homes.

Do these millionaires really have the blessings of life "under the sun"? Life is more than a pay package. There are many other things that God teaches us to consider.

It is time for you and your spouse to laugh at each other and enjoy a few moments "under the sun" together.

Do not be fixated on the negatives. There are many things to talk about. Have dinner together! Make tea for each other. Have fun! Enjoy and accept each other's friendship! Do not accuse each other! Play with each other and make light of all the ugliness in your spouse. This world is not our home. We are just passing through and under the sun for a season! Pass your tests of this life under the sun!

5. Eat of your wealth and take your portion as you work.

There is an evil which I have seen under the sun, and it is common among men: A man to whom God hath given riches, wealth, and honour, so that he wanteth nothing for his soul of all that he desireth, yet God giveth him not power to eat thereof, but a stranger eateth it: this is vanity, and it is an evil disease.

Ecclesiastes 6:1-2

Spend money on yourself. Use some of the wealth you have earned on yourself. That is part of enjoying your working life. Invest in your surroundings. If you spend most of your time in your bedroom, make it the nicest bedroom in the world. Have fun with the goodies God has given you. It is an evil thing to be unable to use the wealth you have earned. Failure to eat your portion will make you hate life and hate work.

And I gave my heart to know wisdom, and to know madness and folly: I perceived that this also is vexation of spirit. For in much wisdom is much grief: and he that increaseth knowledge increaseth sorrow.

Ecclesiastes 1:17-18

6. Remember that people are envious of hard-working people.

Again, I considered all travail, and every right work, that for this a man is envied of his neighbour. This is also vanity and vexation of spirit.

Ecclesiastes 4:4

This world has six billion selfish, greedy and lazy people. When a hard-working person comes along, he tills the ground, prospers and creates wealth. Unfortunately, his wealth and success only stir up the jealousy of his brothers.

Abel did not do anything to hurt his brother Cain. Cain was jealous of Abel's success and eventually killed him.

Under the sun, hard-working and successful people will always be surrounded by envious people. Successful men all over the world live under the teeming threat of envious people.

Jesus Christ was crucified because of envy. "For he knew that the chief priests had delivered him for envy" (Mark 15:10).

7. Be content as you work for God.

Better is an handful with quietness, than both the hands full with travail and vexation of spirit.

Ecclesiastes 4:6

This may be one of the most important strengths that you will ever develop. The ability to be content is so important for full-time ministers and their families. It is this ability that keeps your mind and heart on eternity.

In this all-important spiritual state, you will be content with food, clothes and somewhere to live. This truly is the biblical prescription for all spiritual pilgrims.

8. Patience will make you go further.

Better is the end of a thing than the beginning thereof: and the patient in spirit is better than the proud in spirit.

Ecclesiastes 7:8

Impatience is the brother of discontentment. Impatient people cannot wait for the seeds they have sown to germinate. They must have all the money now. They must have cars, houses, gold and other rewards now and in this life. It is this spirit of impatience that cuts us off many a minister from realizing their full potential.

9. Wisdom will make you work better.

This wisdom have I seen also under the sun, and it seemed great unto me:

Ecclesiastes 9:13

Every job can be made easier and faster through wisdom. Farming, carpentry, fishing and even the practice of medicine are much easier today because wisdom has made everything a little easier. Use wisdom to make whatever work you do faster and more fruitful.

10. Working in twos is always more fruitful and enjoyable.

Two are better than one; because they have a good reward for their labour.

Ecclesiastes 4:9

An eternal law of fruitful work is the law of working in teams of twos. I have tried sending out people alone and I have discovered that two are always better than one. Believe and practise the principle of "two are better than one". It will make your life's work much easier.

CHAPTER 10

How to Find Your Life's Work

Your life's work is a gift from God. Many people would be surprised to find out that work is actually a gift from God. Without the gift of work, many would be listless, lacking the energy and vitality of life.

It is the work God has given us to do that energizes us. As soon as you sense that the work you are doing is worthless, it is difficult to continue working. This revelation of how futile secular work is, is what spurs many into full-time ministry.

It is difficult to spend all your energy doing something that you know is a waste of time.

Seven Things You Must Know about Work

1. Know that work is better than rest, because God worked six days and rested one day **(Exodus 20:11).**
2. Understand why too much rest is a negative thing. **(Proverbs 6:10-11)**
3. Know that happiness at work is one of the gifts of God. **(Ecclesiastes 5:19)**
4. Know the things that take away the joy of work. **(Songs 2:15)**

5. It is possible to work without craving for leave. **(John 9:4)**

6. Keep searching till you find your life's work. **(Esther 4:14)**

7. Decide to work rather than to play or to rest. **(Nehemiah 4:6)**

Eight Ways to Identify Your Life's Work

1. Your life's work will give a new meaning to your life.

When you find your life's work, it will give you something more than money. There is more to life than the amount of money you have. King Solomon had all the money in the world yet he said, "Vanity of vanities; all is vanity."

2. Your life's work is something God has called you to.

Jesus saith unto them, My meat is to do the will of him that sent me, and to finish his work.

John 4:34

When I followed the call of God on my life, I found my life's work. Many people live and die without beginning their life's work.

3. Your life's work is something that you will not hate.

Solomon hated his work and his life. This is the futility of those whose work is related only to life on this earth. Solomon was depressed and miserable at the end of his life.

Therefore I hated life; because the work that is wrought under the sun is grievous unto me: for all is vanity and vexation of spirit.

Yea I hated all my labour which I had taken under the sun: because I should leave it unto the man that shall be after me.

Ecclesiastes 2:17-18

Solomon's wisdom was the wisdom *under the sun* - the wisdom for life on this earth. As far as earthly achievements were concerned, Solomon accomplished very much. But as he approached the gates of eternity, his earthly accomplishments paled into insignificance. Work that focuses on eternity will not leave you depressed.

Queen Margaret of Scotland at the end of her life said, "Shame on life!"

However, the missionary, dying on his ship in the midst of the sea said, "I go with the gladness of a boy bounding from school. I feel so strong in Christ."

Since I entered into full-time ministry, I have not hated my work or my life. When I worked in the secular world, I hated work and I found my life useless. A little analysis of those ahead of me showed me the futility of all my labour. O what a blessing it is for me to have found my life's work!

4. In your life's work, you will enjoy the rewards of your labour.

Many people do not enjoy the fruits of their hard work. They work all day and all night but never sit down to enjoy the simple benefits of life.

...every man should eat and drink, and enjoy the good of all his labour, it is the gift of God.

Ecclesiastes 3:13

The gift of God enables you to be happy, enjoy the little pleasures, and rest from your labours. When you find your life's work you will experience all these.

5. In your life's work, money will no longer drive you.

When you find your life's work, money will not matter so much anymore. You will work for the joy of fulfilling God's will.

Like Jesus, you will say, "My meat (satisfaction) is to do the will of Him that sent me."

You will also know that a man's life does not consist in the abundance of things that he possesses (Luke 12:15). You will know that money is elusive and no one ever has enough.

> **He that loveth silver shall not be satisfied with silver; nor he that loveth abundance with increase: this is also vanity.**
>
> **Ecclesiastes 5:10**

6. In your life's work you will not labour in vain.

Working in the world is vanity. Solomon told us that repeatedly. It is working in the Lord that is not vanity. Paul described his work differently. Solomon called his work vanity but Paul said his work was not in vain.

> **Therefore, my beloved brethren, be ye stedfast, unmoveable, always abounding in the work of the Lord, forasmuch as ye know that your labour is not in vain in the Lord.**
>
> **1 Corinthians 15:58**

7. Your life's work makes you become a blessing to others.

As you fulfil God's calling, you will become a blessing to others. God will bless you abundantly and you will help many people.

> **I have shewed you all things, how that so labouring ye ought to support the weak, and to remember the words of the Lord Jesus, how he said, It is more blessed to give than to receive.**
>
> **Acts 20:35**

8. In your life's work your talents will be revealed.

When I worked in the secular world, most of the gifts God had given me were submerged. I was never a leader, I was never appointed to any special position and I did not shine.

In full-time ministry, my abilities and talents have been utilized to the full. I have found a job that taxes my mind and my strength to the uttermost. Working in full-time ministry makes my sleep enjoyable.

The sleep of a labouring man is sweet, whether he eat little or much: but the abundance of the rich will not suffer him to sleep.

Ecclesiastes 5:12

CHAPTER 11

Why Some People Do Not Prosper at Work

Some people do not prosper because they are in the wrong job. Even when you are diligent and hardworking, being in a job you are not suited for will destroy you. You will not shine and you will not excel because you are not born for the kind of job you have chosen.

1. You cannot prosper without a calling.

When you are not called to something, you get into all sorts of difficulties. A train is not designed to fly. No matter how it is positioned on the runway, flying is impossible! It was designed to stay on the ground and to move along rail tracks.

It is important that you find your calling because you are designed to do specific things. Many difficulties come from doing jobs that you are not suited for. Functioning in a call which is not your own is like taking an honour which is not yours.

And no man taketh this honour unto himself, but he that is called of God...

Hebrews 5:4

2. You cannot prosper with the wrong temperament.

Perhaps this is one of the most important points in this book. In a previous chapter we discussed how each temperament is suited for certain jobs. Make sure that you are doing a job suited to your particular temperament. If you are a choleric person, find a leadership job that is suitable for choleric people. If you are phlegmatic, ask to be excused from jobs that require a driving, leadership personality!

It is in your interest that you work according to your particular temperament. If you do not, you will repeatedly be regarded as a failure.

3. You cannot prosper in the wrong company.

If you do not have to sit with sinners all day long, you are truly blessed. Pray that God will give you people whose company you enjoy.

Blessed is the man that walketh not in the counsel of the ungodly, nor standeth in the way of sinners, nor sitteth in the seat of the scornful.

Psalms 1:1

4. You cannot prosper in a meaningless job.

Then I looked on all the works that my hands had wrought, and on the labour that I had laboured to do: and, behold, all was vanity and vexation of spirit, and there was no profit under the sun.

Ecclesiastes 2:11

It is unfortunate to have to do a meaningless job. During the Second World War, one of the punishments given to intelligent professors and scientists was the carrying of rocks from one end of a prison yard to the other.

From morning until evening, they carried these rocks to and fro, creating a heap and then taking it apart when it reached a certain height. It was indeed a sore vexation to these honourable men. Some of them went crazy as they did years and years of this meaningless work. Perhaps that is why you are going crazy at your current job.

5. You cannot prosper working for someone you dislike.

Surely oppression maketh a wise man mad; and a gift destroyeth the heart.

Ecclesiastes 7:7

It is a painful experience to work for someone you dislike. It is truly a joy to work for someone whose company and leadership you enjoy. I pray that you will find an opportunity to work for someone who does not oppress you.

6. You cannot prosper without a proper preparation.

Prepare thy work without, and make it fit for thyself in the field; and afterwards build thine house.

Proverbs 24:27

The lack of preparation makes work a very difficult thing. Preparation is necessary for every job. Sometimes you have not read your notes or prepared adequately. A lack of preparation makes you incapable of your tasks.

This lack of preparation makes work a difficult experience everyday. It is important to prepare yourself adequately so that you will find yourself enjoying the work God has given you.

CHAPTER 12

How to Have Favour with Your Boss

1. **See him as one who is placed there by God.**

   ...For there is no authority except from God, and those which exist are established by God.
   Romans 13:1

2. **Recognize and relate to him as you would relate with God Himself.**

   Do your work as though you are doing it for the Lord.

   ...with good will doing service, as to the Lord, and not to men:
   Ephesians 6:7

3. **Be humble towards your boss.**

   Humility is the only way to promotion in God's house.

   And whosoever will be chief among you, let him be your servant:
   Matthew 20:27

4. Learn all you can about your job.

A wise man will hear, and will increase learning; and a man of understanding shall attain unto wise counsels

Proverbs 1:5

There is a lot to learn every day. We will never stop learning until we die. Open your heart and discover all there is to know about your job.

5. Listen to instructions carefully.

Recognize that the person in authority over you knows something that you don't. That is why he is in that position.

Hear, ye children, the instruction of a father, and attend to know understanding.

Proverbs 4:1

6. Understand the spirit of the instruction.

Long-winded meetings and lengthy discussions are intended to make you understand your instructions. When you understand the spirit of the instruction, you are able to carry out your orders better.

7. Discover what your boss likes and wants, then do it!

There are certain things that please every important person. They often do not care about many things. Often they look out for just one thing and if you can get that right, you will always be in their good books.

Surprisingly, people do a hundred different things that have not been asked for and leave out the one thing that means everything to the boss.

8. Learn what displeases your boss and avoid those things like the plague.

Notice what angers your boss and learn to avoid them. Understand why he is upset by certain things and discover what to do to avoid them. Like I said, it takes very little to please important people. They do not have time for many things. There are just a few things they notice.

9. Learn to anticipate your boss's next move.

How refreshing it is to have a servant who knows what you will do next. It is like a cool drink on a very hot and sunny day. Anticipating your boss's next move is to think the way he thinks and to plan with him in mind. This ability to anticipate things shows a good level of intelligence and is also a sign of partnership.

10. Repeat his instructions to be sure you understand them.

When you receive instructions, develop a habit of repeating what you have heard to make sure you got it right. Sometimes, a slight variation in understanding the instruction can lead to a disaster.

11. Start writing when your boss starts speaking.

This shows you are smart, intelligent and ready for action. Always have a book ready when he calls. There may be nothing to write, but you must be ready. It is discouraging to give a lot of instructions only to find that nothing has been written by a scatter-brained employee.

12. Do not be jumbled up and confused in his presence.

It is important to be composed and ready for every task. Have your note book and pen at hand at all times so that you do not look silly and disorganized.

13. Be dressed properly and decently whenever he is present.

Throw away clothes that are unacceptable and inappropriate so that even in your most casual moments you will be professional and ready for action.

14. Do what you are asked to do immediately.

There is no better time to start carrying out an instruction than right now. Start immediately! Carry out new instructions first and do routine things later. Your boss's heart will warm up to you when you deal with his urgent requests.

15. Never stop routine jobs until instructed.

Some routine activities will never be checked unless there is some problem or other. Often, it is in a time of crisis that the negligence of routine work is discovered. This is the point at which many people lose their jobs.

16. Carry out all instructions to their logical conclusion.

Every boss wants to hear that the mission is accomplished. No supervisor wants to be told about unsolved problems.

He wants to hear about solutions. He wants to hear how you overcame the obstacles you met. Within one command lies a host of challenges that must be overcome. Every boss is looking for problem solvers. Everyone can narrate a string of unsolved problems but who can solve them?

Solve any problems that come up in the course of doing your job. Just make sure you bring your instructions to a thorough conclusion.

17. Become your boss's no.1 problem solver.

Every boss is attracted to solution-bringers, bridge-builders, problem solvers and accomplishers. Never leave unsolved a problem that you could have solved. The one thing that will devalue you in your boss' eyes is when you do not solve problems. Most bosses know that there are a host of problems to be overcome. That is the very reason why he gave you the job.

18. Never criticize your boss publicly or privately.

It will erode your spiritual relationship with him and open the door for demons. Ask the Israelites what happened to them when they began complaining about Moses. A grumbling employee is a liability and I would advise any leader to dismiss all the grumblers.

19. At all costs, avoid the job of the "office complainer".

There are always people who are not happy about something. They have a chronic spirit of murmuring. Make sure you never become the "office complainer".

20. Never be angry or irritated at new instructions.

Do not be upset when instructions are changed. Do not be angry when instructions are repeated. Your job is to be humble and do what you are told. If you get irritated at a change of instructions, you are probably too big for your job.

21. Humbly receive all corrections no matter how long you have been around.

The longer you stay in a job, the more likely you are to think that you know everything. Humble yourself and receive correction. You may have been around for ten years but there are still things to learn.

22. Be spiritual, be restful and be wise.

When you do not use your time wisely, you never have time to pray. It is important to be prayerful and restful. It makes you wiser and more effective. When you are not restful, you become incomplete, inconclusive and untidy. Watch out! Redeem the time because the days are evil.

Redeeming the time, because the days are evil.

Ephesians 5:16

Spiritual leaders always know those around them who are not spiritual.